Collins

真正上海数学

Real Shanghai Mathematics

3.2

Pupil Textbook

世纪出版

上海教育出版社
SHANGHAI EDUCATIONAL
PUBLISHING HOUSE

MIX
Paper from responsible sources
FSC™ C007454

This book is produced from independently certified FSC paper to ensure responsible forest management.

For more information visit: **www.harpercollins.co.uk/green**

William Collins' dream of knowledge for all began with the publication of his first book in 1819. A self-educated mill worker, he not only enriched millions of lives, but also founded a flourishing publishing house. Today, staying true to this spirit, Collins books are packed with inspiration, innovation and practical expertise. They place you at the centre of a world of possibility and give you exactly what you need to explore it.

Collins. Freedom to teach.

Collins
An imprint of HarperCollins*Publishers*
The News Building
1 London Bridge Street
London
SE1 9GF

Browse the complete Collins catalogue at
www.collins.co.uk

10 9 8 7 6 5 4

ISBN 978-0-00-826169-6

The educational materials in this book were compiled in accordance with the course curriculum produced by the Shanghai Schools (Pre-Schools) Curriculum Reform Commission and 'Maths Syllabus for Shanghai Schools (Trial Implementation)' for use in Primary 3 Second Term under the nine-year compulsory education system.

These educational materials were compiled by the head of Shanghai Normal University, and reviewed and approved for trial use by Shanghai Schools Educational Materials Review Board.

The writers for this book's educational materials are:

Editor-in-Chief: Jianhong Huang
Guest Writers (Listed by Chinese character strokes in surname): Ye Wei, Tong Hui, Song Yongfu, Ju Lihua, Xu Peijing, Huang Jianhong

This volume's Practice Book was revised by: 'Primary School Maths Practice Book' Compilation Team

British Library Cataloguing in Publication Data
A catalogue record for this publication is available from the British Library.

For the English edition:

Primary Publishing Director: Lee Newman
Primary Publishing Managers: Fiona McGlade, Lizzie Catford
Editorial Project Manager: Mike Appleton
Editorial Manager: Amanda Harman
Editorial Assistant: Holly Blood
Managing Translator: Huang Xingfeng
Translators: Huang Chunhua, Lin Xumai, Shi Jiamin, Tang Xiaofen, Yang Lili, Ye Huini, Zhang Rongxi, Zhou Yi
Lead Editor: Tanya Solomons
Copyeditor: Joan Miller
Proofreaders: Jan Schubert, Helen Bleck, Joan Miller
Cover artist: Amparo Barrera
Designer: Ken Vail Graphic Design
Production Controller: Sarah Burke
Printed and bound by CPI Group (UK) Ltd, Croydon, CR0 4YY

All images with permission from Shanghai Century Publishing Group.

Contents

Unit One
Revising and improving

Brief revision

 Calculate these number sentences, then find and shade the answer the same colour as its number sentence. What picture can you see?

32 × 3 =	288 ÷ 6 × 7 =	809 ÷ 4 =
76 × 8 =	98 ÷ 7 =	563 ÷ 8 =
936 ÷ 3 =	132 × 2 + 431 =	83 × 3 =
4 × 327 =	444 ÷ 5 =	858 ÷ 6 + 158 =
222 × 7 ÷ 6 =	788 ÷ 4 − 89 =	1214 ÷ 6 =
357 × 3 =	764 − 83 × 6 =	47 + 213 × 3 =
3066 ÷ 7 ÷ 6 =	26 × 4 =	527 × 4 − 1888 =
420 ÷ 6 =	43 × 8 × 3 =	938 ÷ 7 − 45 =

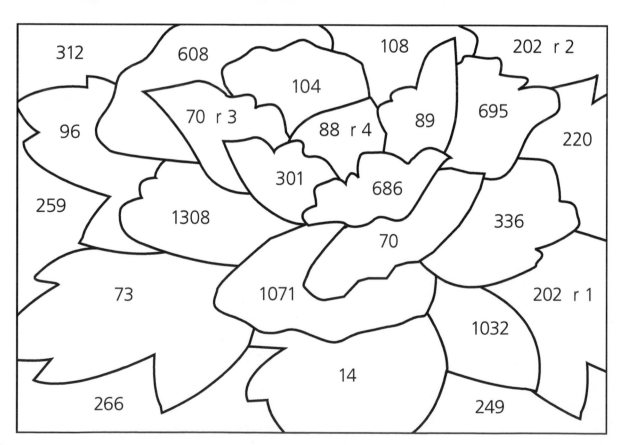

Four arithmetic operations with brackets

Example

There are 48 kg of food. The cow eats 15 kg of it. The three horses share the rest equally. How many kilograms of food does each horse eat?

There are 48 kg of food and 15 kg have been eaten. The amount left is:

48 − 15 = 33 (kg)

Each horse eats:

33 ÷ 3 = 11 (kg)

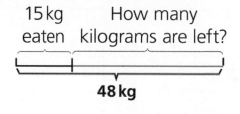

15 kg eaten — How many kilograms are left?

48 kg

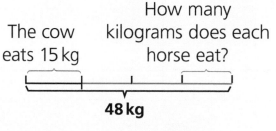

The cow eats 15 kg — How many kilograms does each horse eat?

48 kg

Write Dylan's calculation method as a number sentence.

(48 − 15) ÷ 3
= 33 ÷ 3
= 11 (kg)

Because you must calculate 48 − 15 first, you should add brackets. The part in brackets is calculated first.

Answer: Each horse eats ▨ kg of food.

Practice

497 ÷ (26 − 19)   (248 + 56) ÷ 8   345 ÷ (27 ÷ 9)

Estimating area (1)

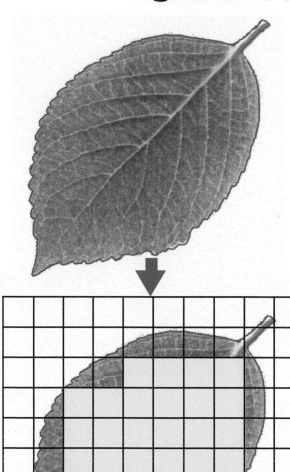

What is the area of this leaf?

Put the leaf under a clear centimetre squared grid.

There are 31 whole squares. But what about the rest?

Count the squares where the leaf fills half or more than half of the square. Don't count the squares where the leaf fills less than half of the square.

 1 cm

We have counted.

Whole squares:

Half or more than half filled squares:

The area of the leaf is approximately: ☐ cm².

Area of compound shapes
Children's playground

Example

What is the area of the children's playground?

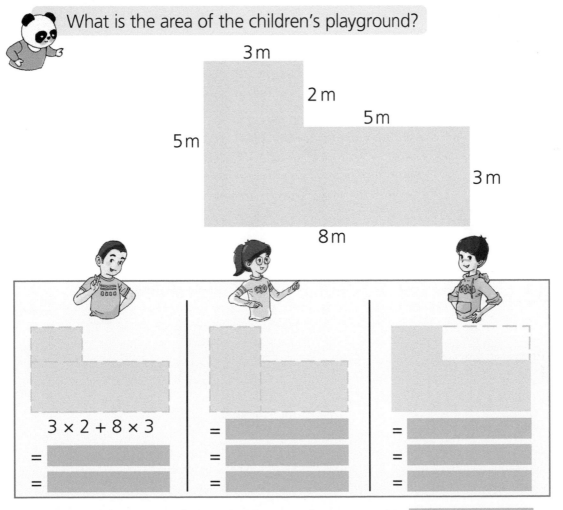

$3 \times 2 + 8 \times 3$

$=$

$=$

$=$

$=$

$=$

$=$

Answer: The area of the children's playground is   .

Practice

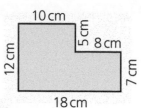

1. **There are three methods of calculating the area of this shape.**

a. 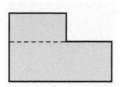   b. 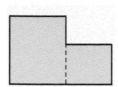   c.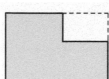

   Fill in the blanks and calculate the shape's area, using each of the methods shown in the diagrams above.

   a. 5 × ▢ + 7 × 18 = ▢

   b. 12 × 10 + ▢ × 8 = ▢

   c. ▢ × 18 – 5 × 8 = ▢

2. **Calculate the area of the shaded part of each shape.**

a. 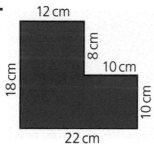   b. 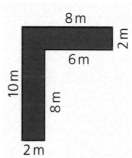   c.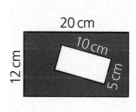

3. **Calculate the area of the shaded part of each shape.**

a. 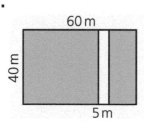   b.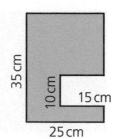

Unit Two
Multiplying and dividing by a two-digit number

Speed, time and distance

You are so slow! I only ran for 6 minutes.

432 m

544 m

I also ran for 8 minutes.

I ran for 8 minutes.

432 m

Example 1

 Who ran the fastest?

 Bull took less time than Bear to run the same distance. So, Bull ran faster than Bear.

Elephant and Bear ran for the same amount of time, but Elephant ran further. So, Elephant ran faster than Bear.

 How can we work out who ran faster, Elephant or Bull?

We can compare how many metres they each ran in one minute.

 The distance travelled per minute (or second, or hour) is called **speed**.

Bear's speed is: 432 ÷ 8 = 54 m/min
'54 m/min' means Bear travelled 54 metres every minute. You read it as '54 metres per minute'.

Elephant's speed is ▨ ⬤ ▨ = ▨ , which you read as:

Bull's speed is ▨ ⬤ ▨ = ▨ , which you read as:

Answer: ▨▨▨▨▨

Example 2

Train A travels 444 km in 3 hours and train B travels 332 km in 2 hours. Which train travels faster?

How far do they travel per hour?

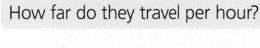

Train A	Train B

 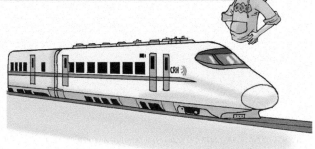

▨▨▨ ⬤ ▨▨ = ▨▨   ▨▨▨ ⬤ ▨▨ = ▨▨

Answer: ▨▨▨▨▨

We can work out the speed like this:

Speed = ▨▨ ⬤ ▨▨

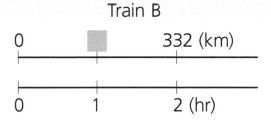

2 Multiplying and dividing by a two-digit number

Try it out!

1. Read about these different speeds.

about 4 km/h

about 16 km/h

about 700 m/min

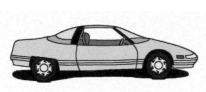

about 2 km/min

about 200 m/sec

about 8500 m/sec

2. Calculate the speeds.

If it travels 3824 m in 8 mins, its speed is ⬜ m/min

If it travels 196 m in 7 secs, its speed is ⬜ m/sec

If it travels 152 km in 4 hrs, its speed is ⬜ km/h

3. Do it yourself.

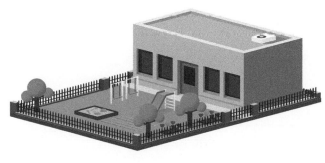

It is ▢ metres around the edge of your school's playground. It takes you about ▢ minutes to walk around it. Your walking speed is about ▢.

Example 3

The speed of a cheetah is 31 m/sec. How far can it run in 7 seconds?

'31 m/sec' means it can run 31 metres per second.

```
0    31                              ▢        m
├────┼────┼────┼────┼────┼────┼────┼────┼
0    1    2    3    4    5    6    7    sec
```

▢ ● ▢ = ▢   Answer: ▢▢▢▢▢▢

We can work out the distance like this:

Distance = ▢ ● ▢

Example 4

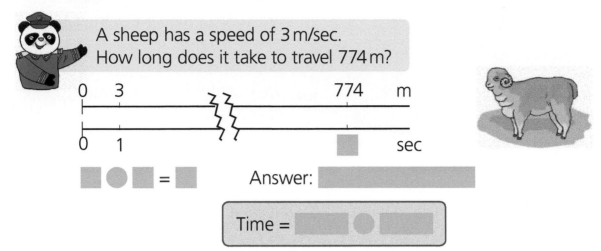

A sheep has a speed of 3 m/sec.
How long does it take to travel 774 m?

0   3   774   m

0   1   ▢   sec

▢ ● ▢ = ▢   Answer: ▬▬▬

Time = ▬ ● ▬

Practice

Fill in the blanks.

Distance		376 km	4760 m	
Time	9 sec	2 hr		12 min
Speed	340 m/s		8 m/s	60 m/min

Multiplying a two-digit number by a multiple of 10

Example

The animal sports tournament is about to begin!

Monkey is cycling from his home to the stadium. How far is the stadium from his home?

92 m/min

It takes 30 minutes from 7 o'clock to half past 7.

$30 \times 92 = \boxed{}$

I calculate by deriving.

$3 \times 92 = 276$

$30 \times 92 = 2760$

'Deriving' means starting with a calculation that you can do easily and using what you know to find the answer you need.

Try it out!

Use Emma's method to calculate.

$2 \times 43 = $	$18 \times 5 = $	$6 \times 91 = $	$72 \times 6 = $
$20 \times 43 = $	$18 \times 50 = $	$60 \times 91 = $	$72 \times 60 = $
$200 \times 43 = $	$18 \times 500 = $	$600 \times 91 = $	$72 \times 600 = $

Practice

There are 20 boxes of juice and 20 boxes of water in the athletes' lounge. Each box contains either 18 bottles of juice or 24 bottles of water. How many more bottles of water are there than bottles of juice in the athletes' lounge?

Multiplying a two-digit number by a two-digit number
Example 1

Look! It's the hedgehog race!

 Here come the hedgehogs! They are running in 14 lanes. Each lane has 12 hedgehogs in it. How many hedgehogs are taking part in the race?

$$14 \times 12 = ?$$

 Estimate first. Approximately how many hedgehogs take part in the race?

$$14 \times 10 = 140$$

Let me estimate it.

The number of hedgehogs that take part in the race is more than (but close to) 140.

 $$14 \times 12 = \boxed{}$$

Let's talk about the calculation method.

I do it like this: 12 = 3 × 4
I multiply 14 by 3, and then by 4.

14 × 12
= 14 × 3 × 4
= 42 × 4
= 168

I do it like this: 12 = 10 + 2
First calculate 14 × 10, then add 14 × 2.

14 × 12
= 14 × 10 + 14 × 2
= 140 + 28
= 168

I do it like this: 14 = 20 − 6
First calculate 20 × 12, then subtract 6 × 12

14 × 12
= 20 × 12 − 6 × 12
= 240 − 72
= 168

I do it like this: 14 = 5 + 9
First calculate 5 × 12, then add 9 × 12

14 × 12
= 5 × 12 + 9 × 12
= 60 + 108
= 168

Answer:

Example 2

How can we calculate 43 × 37?

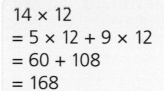

I like Alex's method.

Alex's method: 43 × 37
= 43 × 30 + 43 × 7
= 1290 + 301
= 1591

Let's use Alex's method.

17 × 29
= 17 × 20 + 17 ×
=
=

47 × 73
= 47 ×   + 47 ×
=
=

53 × 67
=
=
=

Example 3

 We can also use the column method.

I do it like this:

```
    4 3
  ×  3 7
  ─────
  3 0 1
```
→
```
    4 3
  ×  3 7
  ─────
  3 0 1
  1 2 9 0
```
→
```
    4 3
  ×  3 7
  ─────
  3 0 1
  1 2 9 0
  ─────
  1 5 9 1
```

First, 43 is multiplied by 7, which is in the ones place.

Next, 43 is multiplied by 3, which is in the tens place.

Finally, add the products together.

This is usually written as:

7 multiplied by 43…

30 multiplied by 43…

```
        4 3
    ×   3 7
    ───────
      3 0 1
    1 2 9 0
    ───────
    1 5 9 1
```

This 0 can be omitted as long as you remember you are multiplying by a multiple of 10.

When a number is multiplied by the digit in the tens place, the end of the product should be aligned with the tens place, even if you omit the zero in the ones place.

Try it out!

Complete these calculations.

$12 × 23 =$

```
     12
  ×  23
  ─────
     36
```

$27 × 23 =$

```
     27
  ×  23
  ─────
     81
```

$55 × 44 =$

```
     55
  ×  44
  ─────
    220
```

Practice

1. Column method

14 × 22 =   16 × 22 =   78 × 22 =

68 × 24 =   68 × 46 =   68 × 68 =

2. Animal hospital

The medicine for these animals has been calculated incorrectly! Please put the calculations right, to make the animals better.

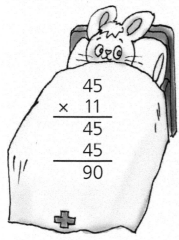

```
  45
× 11
----
  45
  45
----
  90
```

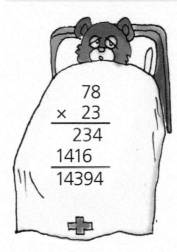

```
   78
 × 23
-----
  234
 1416
-----
14394
```

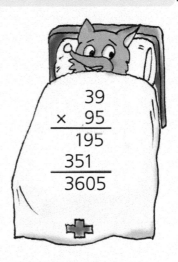

```
   39
 × 95
-----
  195
  351
-----
 3605
```

The correct calculation:
```
  45
× 11
```

The correct calculation:
```
  78
× 23
```

The correct calculation:
```
  39
× 95
```

3. Write number sentences and calculate the answers.

a. What is the product of two 46s multiplied together?

b. What is the sum of eighteen 79s?

Multiplying a two-digit number by a three-digit number

Example 1

 How many cartons of milk did the squirrel deliver for the animal athletes?

28 boxes in all

112 cartons per box

28 × 112 =

30 × 112 = 3360

Let me estimate!

The number of cartons that the squirrel delivered is less than (but close to) 3360.

 How can we calculate 28 × 112?

I calculate like this:

28 × 112
= 20 × 112 + 8 × 112
= 2240 + 896
= 3136

The column method is written like this:

```
      1 1 2
  ×     2 8
  ─────────
      8 9 6   ...  112 multiplied by 8
    2 2 4     ...  112 multiplied by 20
  ─────────
    3 1 3 6
```

Try it out!

124 × 12 =	376 × 34 =	25 × 333 =
124	376	333
× 12	× 34	× 25
————	————	————

Practice

1. Use the column method.

427 × 32 =   54 × 807 =   739 × 25 =

503 × 24 =   12 × 465 =   435 × 36 =

2. Elephant wants to buy 19 boxes of milk. Each box costs £26. Is £456 enough?

3. Hedgehog wants to buy some yogurt snacks. The original price was £17 per box. Now, the price is £11. How much money will Hedgehog save if she buys 168 boxes?

Example 2

The track is 200 metres long. Monkey rides round the track 150 times every week. How many metres does Monkey ride every week?

$$150 \times 200 = \boxed{}$$

How can we calculate 150×200?

Alex's calculation method:

150×200
$= 150 \times 2 \times 100$
$= 300 \times 100$
$= 30\,000$

I calculate by deriving.

Dylan's calculation method:

$15 \times 2 = 30$
$150 \times 2 = 300$
$150 \times 200 = 30\,000$

How can we use the column method to calculate this?

Emma's calculation method:

```
      1 5 0
  ×     2 0 0
  ───────────
  3 0 0 0 0
```

Let me try.

I like Emma's calculation method. Calculate 15 × 2 = 30 first, and then write three zeros at the end of 30 to make it 30 000.

Answer:

There are 3 zeros in total at the end of the two factors, so there must be 3 zeros at the end of the product.

Try it out!

Use Emma's method to complete these calculations.

150 × 40 =   160 × 400 =   180 × 260 =   300 × 240 =

```
   150
×   40
──────
```

```
   160
×  400
──────
```

Practice

You are 19 kilometres away from the sports arena. You want to get to a weightlifting competition there, which will begin in 20 minutes.

Which of these vehicles could you use to get to the arena? Explain your reasoning.

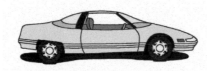

1000 m/min   2000 m/min   700 m/min

Dividing a two-digit number or a three-digit number by a multiple of 10

Example

Before the weightlifting competition, Cow and Sheep were weighing themselves.

My mass is 82 kg.

My mass is 30 kg.

How many times as heavy as Sheep is Cow?
How many kilograms are left over?

We need to calculate how many 30s are in 82.

$$82 \div 30 = \boxed{}$$

How many 30s are there in 82? Let me try.

Dylan's calculation method:

$2 \times 30 < 82$
$3 \times 30 > 82$
there are two 30s in 82
$82 \div 30$ quotient is 2
$82 \div 30 = 2$ r 22

Emma's calculation method:

$8 \div 3$ quotient is 2
$82 \div 30$ quotient is 2
$82 \div 30 = 2$ r 22

How many 30s are there in 82? I calculate by deriving:
How many 3s are there in 8?

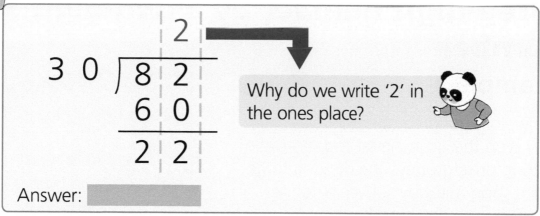

```
          2
  3 0 | 8  2
        6  0
      ---------
        2  2
```

Why do we write '2' in the ones place?

Answer:

Try it out!

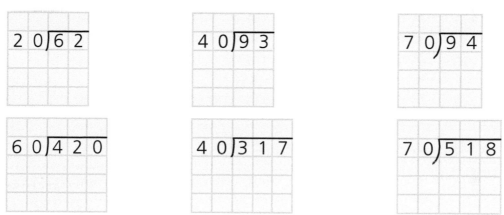

```
  2 0 ) 6 2
```

```
  4 0 ) 9 3
```

```
  7 0 ) 9 4
```

```
  6 0 ) 4 2 0
```

```
  4 0 ) 3 1 7
```

```
  7 0 ) 5 1 8
```

Practice

1. Column method

$97 \div 30$ $\qquad$ $170 \div 30$ $\qquad$ $252 \div 30$

2. Write the number sentences and calculate the answers.

a. How many 60s are there in 540?

b. Divide 492 by 80. What is the quotient and what is the remainder?

Dividing a two-digit number or a three-digit number by a two-digit number

Example 1

The weightlifting competition was over. Cow won the gold medal and received £296 in prize money. She decided to go to the shop and buy souvenirs for her coach, her parents and her friends.

 There were two types of souvenir in the shop. One cost £32, the other cost £37. Cow chose one type of souvenir to buy, and used exactly all the prize money. Which kind of souvenir did she buy? How many souvenirs did she buy?

If she bought the souvenirs costing £32 …

$$296 \div 32 = 9 \text{ (souvenirs) } r\ 8\ (£)$$

$$
\begin{array}{r}
9 \\
32\overline{)296} \\
288 \\
\hline
8
\end{array}
$$ … 9×32

How many 32s are there in 296? Think about it: How many 30s are there in 296? There are nine 30s in 296. $9 \times 32 = 288$. The remainder, 8, is less than the divisor, so 9 is the right quotient.

 Is that right?

 She could buy 9 souvenirs with £8 left over. So, Cow didn't buy the souvenirs that cost £32.

Try it out!

$$26\overline{)52} \qquad 26\overline{)78} \qquad 83\overline{)499} \qquad 83\overline{)678}$$

If she bought souvenirs that cost £37 …

$$296 \div 37 = 8 \text{ (souvenirs)}$$

$$37\overline{)\,296}$$
$$333$$

How many 37s are there in 296? Think about it: How many 30s are there in 296? $9 \times 30 = 270$ so there are nine 30s in 296. But $9 \times 37 = 333$ and $333 > 296$; the quotient 9 is too large, so change it to 8.

$$\begin{array}{r} 8 \\ 37\overline{)\,296} \\ 296 \\ \hline 0 \end{array}$$ ⋯ 8×37

$8 \times 37 = 296$, so 8 is the right quotient.

Which kind of souvenir did she buy? How many souvenirs did she buy?

Answer:

Try it out!

$$27\overline{)\,81}$$

$$28\overline{)\,74}$$

$$29\overline{)\,91}$$

$$76\overline{)\,658}$$

$$87\overline{)\,736}$$

$$88\overline{)\,606}$$

Practice

1. Column method

$89 \div 28$ $\qquad$ $135 \div 27$ $\qquad$ $483 \div 68$

$54 \div 28$ $\qquad$ $108 \div 27$ $\qquad$ $367 \div 68$

2. Animal hospital

The medicine for these animals has been calculated incorrectly! Please put the calculations right, to make the animals better.

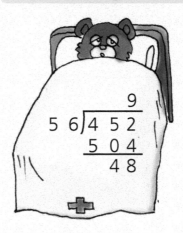

The correct calculation:

$26\overline{)78}$

The correct calculation:

$56\overline{)452}$

The correct calculation:

$45\overline{)350}$

3. If Cow used £296 to buy toys that cost £34 each, how many toys could she buy? How much money would be left over? How many watches costing £78 each could she buy?

Example 2

Cow won the weightlifting gold medal. Butterfly went to Cow's house to congratulate her.

Butterfly took 39 seconds to get to Cow's house. How fast did Butterfly fly?

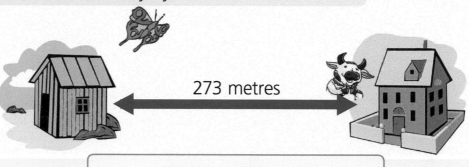

273 metres

$$273 \div 39 = 7$$

$$
\begin{array}{r}
\overset{8}{\cancel{9}} \\
39\overline{)273} \\
351
\end{array}
\longrightarrow
\begin{array}{r}
\overset{7}{\cancel{8}} \\
39\overline{)273} \\
312
\end{array}
$$

How many 39s are there in 273? Think about it: How many 30s are there in 273? There are nine 30s in 273. 9 × 39 > 273 so the quotient 9 is too large. Change it to 8. 8 × 39 > 273; the quotient 8 is still too large, so change it to 7.

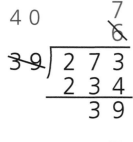

The quotient had to be changed twice. That's quite complicated.

I think of 39 as 40 to find the quotient.

$$
\begin{array}{r}
40 \qquad \overset{7}{\cancel{6}} \\
\cancel{39}\overline{)273} \\
234 \\
39
\end{array}
$$

How many 39s are there in 273? Think about it: How many 40s are there in 273? There are six 40s in 273. 6 × 39 = 234, and the remainder is 39. The remainder equals the divisor, which means the quotient 6 is too small. Change the quotient to 7. 7 × 39 = 273, so 7 is the correct quotient.

$$
\begin{array}{r}
7 \\
39\overline{)273} \\
273 \\
\hline
0
\end{array}
$$

If the divisor is a two-digit number, we can use the closest multiple of 10 to try to find the quotient.

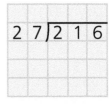

Try it out!

```
2 5 ⟌ 7 1
```

```
2 6 ⟌ 1 8 2
```

```
2 7 ⟌ 2 1 6
```

```
3 5 ⟌ 6 3
```

```
3 6 ⟌ 2 4 2
```

```
3 7 ⟌ 3 0 6
```

```
4 5 ⟌ 1 6 5
```

```
4 6 ⟌ 3 2 2
```

```
4 7 ⟌ 3 6 6
```

Practice

1. Column method

196 ÷ 28	632 ÷ 78	454 ÷ 58
336 ÷ 82	578 ÷ 86	136 ÷ 18

2. Write the number sentence and calculate the answer.

What is 512 divided by 63, 67, 85 and 89 respectively?

Example 3

Giraffe and Elephant love to play basketball and have set up a new club to teach the other animals how to play.

They have saved up some money to buy balls, which cost £12 each.

How many balls can they each buy?

Savings:
Giraffe: £108
Elephant: £96

I'm going to calculate how many balls Giraffe can buy.

$$108 \div 12 = \blacksquare$$

```
           9
   _____
 1 2 ) 1 0 8
       1 0 8
       _____
           0
```

How many 12s are there in 108?
Think about it: How many 10s are there in 108?
There are ten 10s in 108.
$10 \times 12 > 108$
The quotient 10 is too large, so change 10 to 9.
$9 \times 12 = 108$
So 9 is the right quotient.

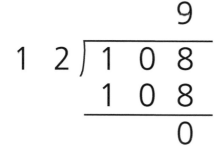 So, what does this tell us?

Answer: Giraffe has enough money to buy ▓▓▓ balls.

I've realised something!
When the digits in the highest digit place of the dividend and divisor are the same, and the number in the first two digit places of the dividend is less than the divisor, we can try 9 as the quotient first.

29

Try it out!

$19\overline{)171}$ $\qquad$ $19\overline{)152}$ $\qquad$ $19\overline{)133}$

$17\overline{)153}$ $\qquad$ $17\overline{)136}$ $\qquad$ $17\overline{)119}$

I'm going to calculate how many balls Elephant can buy with his savings.

$96 \div 12 = \square$

$$\begin{array}{r} 8 \\ \not{9} \\ 12\overline{)\;\;96} \\ 108 \\ \hline \end{array}$$

How many 12s are there in 96?
Think about it: How many 10s are there in 96?
There are nine 10s in 96.
$9 \times 12 > 96$
The quotient 9 is too large, so change 9 to 8.
$8 \times 12 = 96$
So 8 is the right quotient.

$$\begin{array}{r} 8 \\ 12\overline{)96} \\ 96 \\ \hline 0 \end{array}$$

Answer: Elephant has enough money to buy ____ balls.

It takes too long to change the quotient.
I can find the quotient very quickly.

I think:

■ × 12 = 96,

$$12 \overline{\smash{\big)}\ 9\ 6}$$

Write 8 in the ■. So, the quotient should be 8.

If the divisor is small, it is more convenient to try using mental arithmetic to find the quotient.

Try it out!

$$12 \overline{\smash{\big)}\ 8\ 4}$$

$$13 \overline{\smash{\big)}\ 9\ 1}$$

$$16 \overline{\smash{\big)}\ 9\ 6}$$

Practice

Who is the best archer? Complete the table.

	Number of arrows	Total score	Average score per arrow	Rank
Dog	11	44		
Bear	24	192		
Tortoise	18	54		
Deer	14	70		
Cat	19	38		
Horse	17	153		
Cow	22	132		
Monkey	10	100		
Elephant	18	126		

Dividing a multi-digit number by a two-digit number
Example 1

At the end of a football game, the referee awarded the 'Fair Play Award' to The Cubs football team.

132 pencils are shared between 11 players in The Cubs football team. How many pencils does each player get?

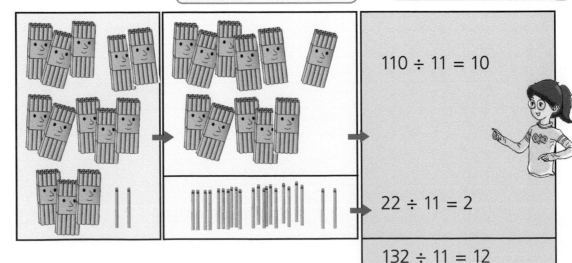

How can we calculate 132 ÷ 11?

$$132 ÷ 11 = \boxed{}$$

Keep 11 boxes of 10 pencils, and split the other two boxes to give 22 single pencils.

$$110 ÷ 11 = 10$$

$$22 ÷ 11 = 2$$

$$132 ÷ 11 = 12$$

We can also use the column method to calculate $132 \div 11$.

The calculation can be written in this way:

```
           1 2
      11 ) 1 3 2
           1 1        ... 10 × 11
           ─────
           2 2
           2 2        ... 2 × 11
           ─────
             0
```

When the divisor is a two-digit number, divide the number in the first two digit places of the dividend first. Write the quotient in the space above the last digit place in the number you divided into. The remainder should be less than the divisor every time.

Try it out!

```
2 0 ) 3 0 0
```

```
2 5 ) 3 0 0
```

```
1 2 ) 3 0 0
```

Practice

1. Use the column method to find the answers.

$528 \div 22$ $514 \div 24$ $600 \div 25$

2. Mr Sea Lion is a reporter for the animal sports competition. He's typing a 576-word press release. If he can type 24 words in one minute, how many minutes does he need to type this press release? If he can type 12 words more per minute, how many minutes would he need then?

Example 2

3780 animals are travelling home by coach after the sports competition.

Please line up and board the coach one by one.

1. If a coach can take 63 animals, how many coaches are needed to take all the animals?

$$3780 \div 63 = \boxed{}$$

Let me work it out!

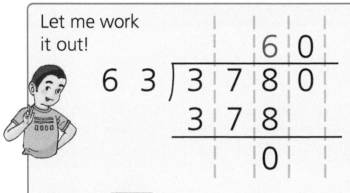

$$
\begin{array}{r}
6\,0 \\
63\,\overline{)\,3\,7\,8\,0\,} \\
3\,7\,8 \\
\hline
0
\end{array}
$$

Why is the '6' in the tens place?

Can I leave out the '0' in the ones place of the quotient?

Answer: _____

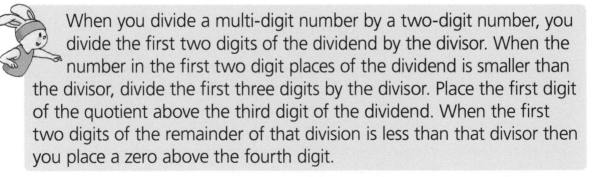

When you divide a multi-digit number by a two-digit number, you divide the first two digits of the dividend by the divisor. When the number in the first two digit places of the dividend is smaller than the divisor, divide the first three digits by the divisor. Place the first digit of the quotient above the third digit of the dividend. When the first two digits of the remainder of that division is less than that divisor then you place a zero above the fourth digit.

Try it out!

Estimate how many digits the quotient has first. Then find the answer.

$$3\,7\,\overline{)\,2\,9\,6\,0}$$

$$2\,8\,\overline{)\,8\,5\,7}$$

$$4\,2\,\overline{)\,2\,5\,5\,1}$$

2. If a coach can take 35 animals, how many coaches are needed to take all the animals? 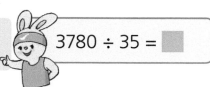 $3780 \div 35 = $ ▦

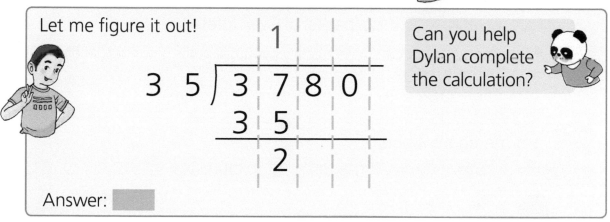

Let me figure it out!

$$\begin{array}{r} 1 \\ 3\,5\,\overline{)\,3\,7\,8\,0} \\ 3\,5 \\ \hline 2 \end{array}$$

Can you help Dylan complete the calculation?

Answer: ▦

Place 0 above the third digit of the dividend because 28 is less than 35.

Try it out!

Estimate how many digits the quotient has first. Then find the answers.

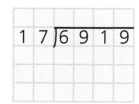
$$1\,7\,\overline{)\,6\,9\,1\,9}$$

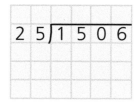
$$2\,5\,\overline{)\,1\,5\,0\,6}$$

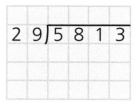
$$2\,9\,\overline{)\,5\,8\,1\,3}$$

Try it out!

Use the column method to complete the calculations.

$638 \div 32$ $967 \div 16$ $8114 \div 27$

Example 3

Mr Dolphin is a sports photographer. He took 364 pictures at the animal sports tournament.

 If you put these pictures into an album with 16 pictures on each page, how many pages would be filled? How many pictures would be left over?

 Let me figure it out!

364 ÷ 16 = 22 (pages) r 8 (pictures)

Let me figure it out!

364 ÷ 16 = 21 (pages) r 28 (pictures)

 Let me figure it out!

364 ÷ 16 = 22 (pages) r 12 (pictures)

Who is right?

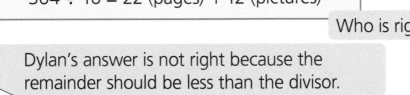 Dylan's answer is not right because the remainder should be less than the divisor.

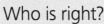 For Emma's and Poppy's answers, the remainders are both less than the divisors. Who is right?

 Remember what you have learned so far. Can you check the division calculation above?

 Use 'quotient × divisor + remainder = dividend' to check the answer.

Because: 22 × 16 + 8 = ☐ ,

22 × 16 + 12 = ☐ ,

So ☐ is right.   Answer:

Try it out!

Use the column method to calculate, then check the answers.

988 ÷ 38   5937 ÷ 84   8017 ÷ 39

Practice exercise

1. Use the column method to complete the calculations.
Check your answers to the questions marked with *.

84×93 $\qquad$ 27×604 $\qquad$ 760×120

$964 \div 28$ $\qquad$ $*2038 \div 19$ $\qquad$ $*4320 \div 24$

2. Write the number sentences and calculate the answers.

a. What is the product of multiplying the two largest two-digit numbers?

b. How many times as great as the largest two-digit number is the largest four-digit number?

3. A calculator costs £25. A computer costs 40 times as much as a calculator. What is the price difference between a computer and a calculator?

4. A road between point A and point B is 576 kilometres long. How long does it take to get from A to B by each mode of transport travelling at the following speeds?

Bike: 16 km/h	Bus: 48 km/h
Motorcycle: 72 km/h	Car: 96 km/h

5. It takes Dylan 24 minutes to walk from home to school. How many minutes would it take him to walk from school to the cinema at the same speed? How many minutes would it take him to walk from home to the cinema at the same speed?

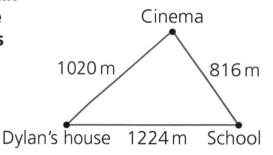

Unit Three
Statistics

Bar charts (2)
Example 1

The numbers of vehicles at the animal sports tournament were recorded.

Type of vehicle	buses	cars	motorcycles	bicycles
Number of vehicles	15	32	24	37

This data can be represented in a bar chart.

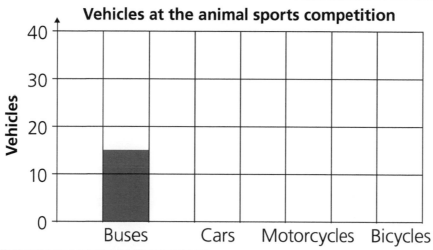

We can also make a bar chart this way around.

Complete the bar chart below.

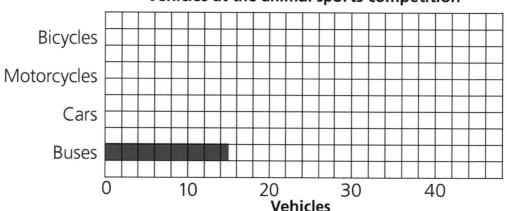

How many vehicles does 1 unit on the horizontal axis represent?

39

Example 2

What is the most popular ice cream flavour sold by these two kiosks?

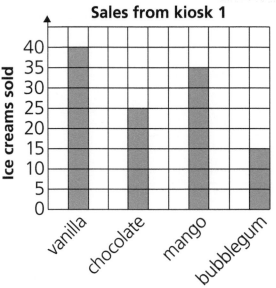

Sales from kiosk 1

Ice creams sold

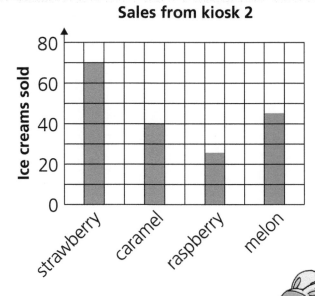

Sales from kiosk 2

Ice creams sold

Look at the two bar charts carefully. What do you notice?

The length of the bar represents the number in the bar chart.
The length of the bar is related to the quantity of 1 space.

Try it out!

Use the data in the table to draw a bar chart.

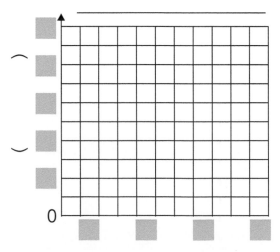

Favourite sports of Year 3 pupils

Favourite sport	football	swimming	running	long jump
Number of pupils	65	40	95	30

Unit Four
Introduction to fractions (1)

Whole and part

If the diagram on the left represents a whole, then the diagram on the right represents part of a whole.

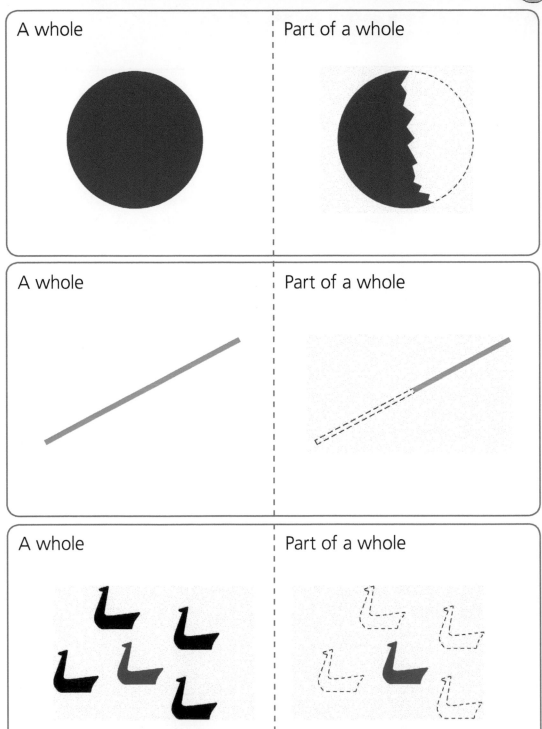

A whole	Part of a whole
A whole	Part of a whole
A whole	Part of a whole

Unit fractions

Example 1: Sharing cakes

1. Dylan and Alex share a cake equally. How much cake do they each get?

If the cake is divided equally, each person gets a half.

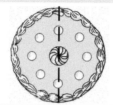 

'Half' can be written as $\frac{1}{2}$. Read it as 'one half' or 'a half'.

2.  A cake is divided into 4 equal pieces for four children.

 Let me divide it.

Emma's method is not right. Everyone should get an equal share of the cake.

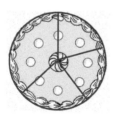

How can we represent the amount of cake each child gets?

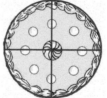

The cake is divided into 4 equal pieces. Each piece is one quarter of the cake.

'One quarter' is written as $\frac{1}{4}$.

Each child gets $\frac{1}{4}$ of the cake.

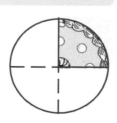

3. 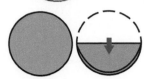 Fold a circle of paper.　　Fold the paper in half!

The paper is folded into two sections of the same size and each is $\frac{1}{2}$ of the circle. The amount is (　　) of the circle.

Fold the paper in half again!

The paper is folded into four sections of equal size and each is $\frac{1}{4}$ of the circle. The amount is (　　) of the circle.

Fold the paper in half again!

The paper is folded into eight sections of the same size and each is (　　) of the circle. The amount is (　　) of the circle.

 A whole is divided into several equal parts; each part of the whole is a unit fraction. Numbers such as $\frac{1}{2}$, $\frac{1}{4}$ and $\frac{1}{8}$ are called fractions.

4.  Talk about the fractions and write down the fraction that represents the shaded part of each shape.

5. Do these fractions represent the shaded parts of these shapes correctly? For each shape, tick (✓) for 'yes' or cross (✗) for 'no'. Explain your reasoning.

$\frac{1}{4}$(　)　　$\frac{1}{5}$(　)　　$\frac{1}{3}$(　)　　$\frac{1}{4}$(　)

Example 2: Dividing a strip of paper

1. If you divide a strip of paper that is 1 metre long into 3 equal parts, how long will each part be?

1 metre

☐ metre

The 1 metre strip of paper can be considered as a whole.

 The 1 metre strip of paper is divided into 3 equal parts. Each part is a third of a metre long.

One third of 1 metre is written as $\frac{1}{3}$m.

2. 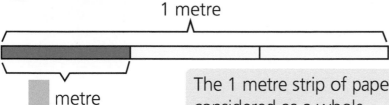 How long is the shaded part of each strip of paper?

1 metre

The purple part is ☐ m.

The red part is ☐ m.

The brown part is ☐ m.

The green part is ☐ m.

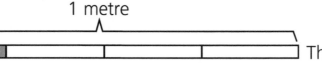 Which is the longest out of $\frac{1}{4}$m, $\frac{1}{5}$m, $\frac{1}{6}$m and $\frac{1}{10}$m? Which is the shortest?

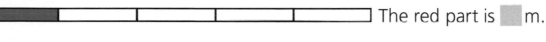 4 is less than 5, but $\frac{1}{4}$ is greater than $\frac{1}{5}$! Because …

What do you notice?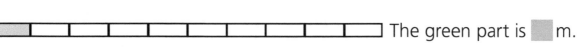

 The more equal parts a whole is divided into, the smaller each part is. The ☐ equal parts a whole is divided into, the ☐ each part is.

Example 3: Sharing sweets

1.

Emma bought a bag of sweets.
She divided all the sweets into 3 piles.

When a bag of sweets is divided equally into 3 piles, each pile of sweets is $\frac{1}{3}$ of the bag of sweets.

2. Write the fraction of items circled in each image.

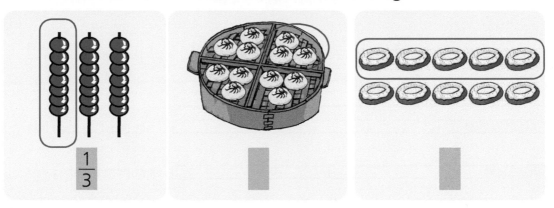

$\frac{1}{3}$

3. Circle the correct number of items for the fraction given.

$\frac{1}{4}$

$\frac{1}{5}$

$\frac{1}{6}$

4. Draw a picture of 12 stars. How many stars is $\frac{1}{4}$ of 12 stars?

Non-unit fractions
Example 1

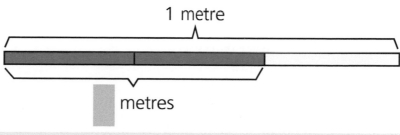

1 metre

 A strip of paper that is 1 metre long is divided equally into 3 pieces. How long are 2 of the pieces together?

☐ metres

The 1 metre strip of paper is divided equally into 3 parts. So, the length of 2 parts is two thirds of 1 metre. Two thirds of 1 metre is written as $\frac{2}{3}$m.

 Divide the whole into 3 parts, so that 2 parts is $\frac{2}{3}$ of the whole.

The length of 1 part is $\frac{1}{3}$m, and the length of 2 parts is $\frac{2}{3}$m.

$\frac{2}{3}$ is two lots of $\frac{1}{3}$.

Example 2

 I want to colour $\frac{3}{4}$m of a strip of paper that is 1 metre long.

Divide the whole into 4 parts, so that 3 parts is $\frac{3}{4}$ of the whole.

The 1 metre strip of paper is divided into 4 equal parts. Each part is $\frac{1}{4}$ of a metre long. 3 parts measure 3 lots of $\frac{1}{4}$ of a metre. That is $\frac{3}{4}$m.

1 metre

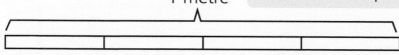

Numbers such as $\frac{2}{3}$ and $\frac{3}{4}$ are also called fractions.

 Two times $\frac{1}{3}$ is $\frac{2}{3}$. Three times $\frac{1}{4}$ is $\frac{3}{4}$. When a whole is divided into several units, more than one of those units put together can be represented as a non-unit fraction.

Example 3

A circle is divided into 4 equal parts.
3 of them make ____ .

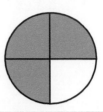

The whole is divided into 4 equal parts. 3 parts is $\frac{3}{4}$ of the whole.

A circle is divided into 4 equal parts.

Each part is $\frac{1}{4}$ of the circle.

3 parts is $\frac{3}{4}$ of the circle.

Example 4

A pack of yogurts is made up of 6 pots. Dylan, Alex, Poppy and Emma each eat a pot of yogurt, so they eat a total of 4 pots. How many packs of yogurts do they eat?

The whole is divided into 6 equal parts, 4 parts is $\frac{4}{6}$ of the whole.

A pack of yogurts is divided into 6 pots.

Each pot is $\frac{1}{6}$ of the pack. 4 people eat 4 lots of $\frac{1}{6}$ of the pack of yogurts, that is $\frac{4}{6}$ of a pack of yogurts.

Practice

1. **For each picture, write the fraction that represents the shaded parts.**

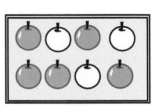

2. Colour the part (or parts) of each picture indicated by the fractions given.

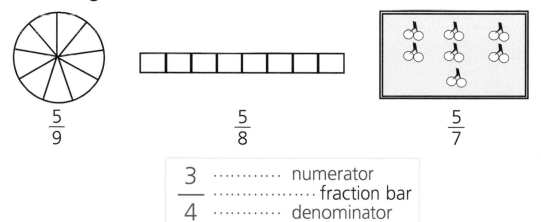

$\dfrac{5}{9}$ $\qquad\qquad$ $\dfrac{5}{8}$ $\qquad\qquad$ $\dfrac{5}{7}$

$$\dfrac{3 \cdots\cdots\cdots \text{numerator}}{4 \cdots\cdots\cdots \text{denominator}} \cdots\cdots\cdots \text{fraction bar}$$

 The denominator of a fraction represents the number of equal parts the whole is divided into, and the numerator indicates how many of the equal parts of the whole are specified.

Example 5

 If each equal part is $\dfrac{1}{5}$ of a metre, how can we describe 2 parts, 3 parts, 4 parts and 5 parts?

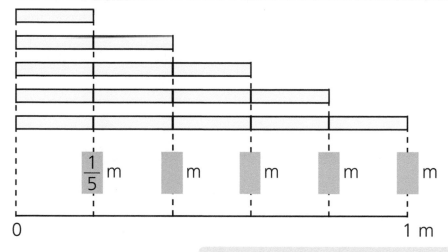

5 lots of $\dfrac{1}{5}$ m is $\dfrac{5}{5}$ m. That is 1 metre.

$\dfrac{5}{5} = 1$

Try it out!

There are 7 candied fruits on a stick. One candied fruit is [____] of a stick of candied fruit. What fraction of a candied fruit stick is 2, 3, 4, 5, 6 or 7 candied fruits?

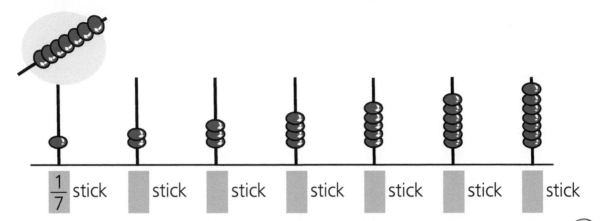

$\frac{1}{7}$ stick   [ ] stick   [ ] stick   [ ] stick   [ ] stick   [ ] stick   [ ] stick

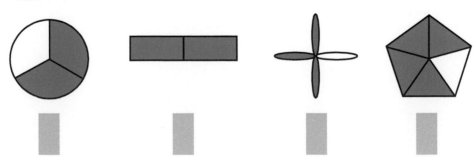

Seven lots of $\frac{1}{7}$ stick is $\frac{7}{7}$ stick. That is 1 stick.

$$\frac{7}{7} = 1$$

Practice

1.

For each shape, write the fraction that represents the shaded part.

[ ]   [ ]   [ ]   [ ]

2. How long is the shaded part of each whole?

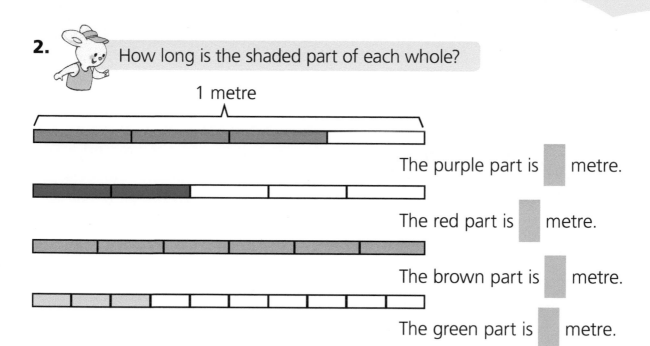

The purple part is ☐ metre.

The red part is ☐ metre.

The brown part is ☐ metre.

The green part is ☐ metre.

3. Circle the correct number of items for the fraction given.

$\frac{3}{4}$

$\frac{4}{5}$

$\frac{5}{6}$

4. Draw a picture of 12 stars. How many stars is $\frac{3}{4}$ of 12 stars?

Unit Five
Calculators

From counting rods to calculators
Example

1. Thousands of years ago, people used counting rods to calculate.

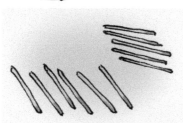

| Vertical form | 1 | 2 | 3 | 4 | 5 | 6 | 7 | 8 | 9 |

| Horizontal form | 1 | 2 | 3 | 4 | 5 | 6 | 7 | 8 | 9 |

The process of calculating 452 + 327 using counting rods is:

| 4 5 2 | 7 5 2 | 7 7 2 | 7 7 9 |

Add 300 first   then add 20   then add 7

2. About 1400 years ago, Chinese people invented the abacus, which helped people to calculate more easily.

Use the abacus to calculate 452 + 327.

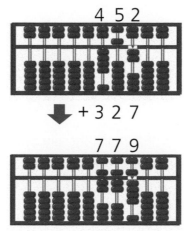

4 5 2

↓ + 3 2 7

7 7 9

3. Nowadays, calculators help us to calculate even faster.

Can you use a calculator to calculate 452 + 327?

Calculator functions
Example 1

 Let's learn about the calculator.

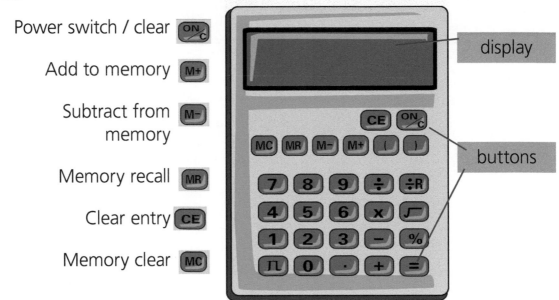

Power switch / clear

Add to memory

Subtract from memory

Memory recall

Clear entry

Memory clear

display

buttons

Try it out!

 Press to turn the calculator on. Then you can use it.

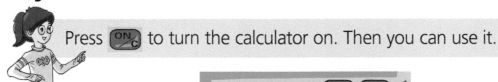

It will automatically switch off if no button is pressed for a while.

You can turn off the power by pressing the OFF button, if the calculator has one.

Example 2

 Turn the calculator on. Then press the buttons in the following order.

 Look at the display. What do you see?

You enter the digits of the number from left to right, so the first digits to be entered have higher place values.

Using a calculator

Example 1

1. Use a calculator to calculate: 2587 + 9604 = ▢

Turn the calculator on. Then press the buttons in the following order.

| 2 | ▶ | 5 | ▶ | 8 | ▶ | 7 |

▶ | + |

▶ | 9 | ▶ | 6 | ▶ | 0 | ▶ | 4 |

▶ | = |

2. Use a calculator to calculate: 80 738 – 31 927 = ▢

Which buttons should you press?

| 8 | ▶ | ▢ | ▶ | ▢ | ▶ | ▢ | ▶ | ▢ |

▶ | ▢ |

▶ | 3 | ▶ | ▢ | ▶ | ▢ | ▶ | ▢ | ▶ | ▢ |

▶ | ▢ |

3. Use a calculator to complete these calculations.

14 596 + 37 625 = ▢   4758 – 3169 = ▢

8848 + 7653 = ▢   8726 – 4698 = ▢

7248 + 50 879 = ▢   32 768 – 18 893 = ▢

4.

How many books are there?

30 240 books in total.

Use a calculator to work out how many stacks of books there are if there are 36 books in each stack.

  =

Answer:

Practice

1. Use a calculator to complete these calculations.

$8 \times 4728 =$	$657 \times 87 =$	$69 \times 148 =$
$1427 \times 18 =$	$156 \times 243 =$	$237 \times 41 =$
$22\,638 \div 98 =$	$7448 \div 76 =$	$17\,216 \div 32 =$
$16\,236 \div 123 =$	$7592 \div 146 =$	$38\,772 \div 1436 =$

2. Use the column method to complete these calculations. Use a calculator to check your answers.

$651 \times 72 =$ ▢

$$\begin{array}{r} 6\ 5\ 1 \\ \times\quad 7\ 2 \\ \hline \end{array}$$

$321 \times 44 =$ ▢

$$\begin{array}{r} 3\ 2\ 1 \\ \times\quad 4\ 4 \\ \hline \end{array}$$

$63 \times 463 =$ ▢

$$\begin{array}{r} 4\ 6\ 3 \\ \times\quad 6\ 3 \\ \hline \end{array}$$

$763 \div 28 =$ ▢

$28\,\overline{)7\ 6\ 3}$

$369 \div 58 =$ ▢

$58\,\overline{)3\ 6\ 9}$

$964 \div 48 =$ ▢

$48\,\overline{)9\ 6\ 4}$

Example 2

During a football league season, Shanghai Stadium admitted 33 086 spectators for the first round, 29 867 spectators for the second round and 30 421 spectators for the third round. How many spectators did Shanghai Stadium admit for the first three rounds?

33 086 + 29 867 + 30 421 = ☐ spectators

Which buttons should you press on the calculator?

☐ ▶ ☐ ▶ ☐ ▶ ☐ ▶ ☐
▶ ☐
▶ ☐ ▶ ☐ ▶ ☐ ▶ ☐ ▶ ☐
▶ ☐
▶ ☐ ▶ ☐ ▶ ☐ ▶ ☐ ▶ ☐
▶ ☐   Answer: ▨

Practice

Find the answers. Then use a calculator to check your answers.

3746 + 12 893 + 9865   89 721 − 34 796 − 43 215

56 347 − 7265 + 18 073   7421 + 83 694 − 37 862

76 × 38 × 29   97 146 ÷ 42 ÷ 9

14 688 ÷ 12 × 307   728 × 54 ÷ 63

Example 3

1.
Start from the **1** button on the calculator and go in an anticlockwise direction. Each set of three buttons makes a three-digit number. Add them together.

123 + 369 + 987 + 741 = ▢

2.
Start from the **1** button on the calculator again and go in a clockwise direction. Each set of three buttons makes a three-digit number. Add them together.

147 + ▢ + ▢ + ▢ = ▢

Compare the answers to the two questions above. What do you notice?

What would happen if you repeated the exercise starting from the **2** button?

Unit Six
Measure and geometry

Perimeter

1. Perimeter

a. A caterpillar crawls around the edge of a leaf.

 The caterpillar crawls once around the edge of the mulberry leaf. The distance the caterpillar crawls is the leaf's perimeter.

b. Trace around the perimeter of each leaf, the carpet and the textbook.

Maple leaf

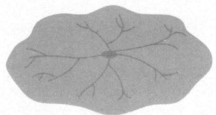

Lotus leaf

Magnolia leaf

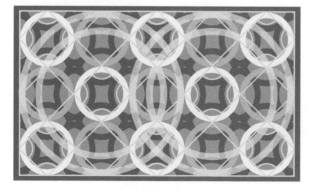

Carpet

The front cover of a textbook

2. Calculate the perimeters of the gardens and the pool.

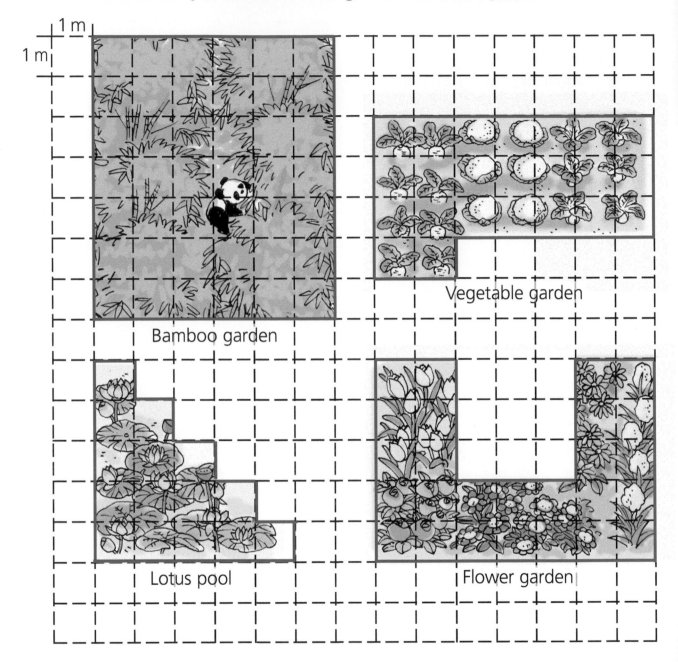

1 m

1 m

Bamboo garden

Vegetable garden

Lotus pool

Flower garden

a. Bamboo garden:

b. Vegetable garden:

c. Lotus pool:

d. Flower garden:

3. Measure and calculate the perimeter of each shape.

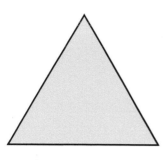

Perimeter:

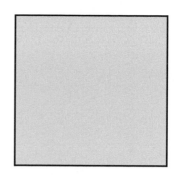

Perimeter:

Perimeter:

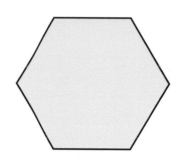

Perimeter:

Calculate the perimeter of each shape.

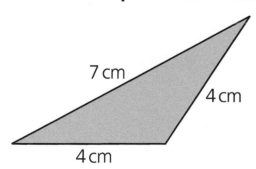

7 cm

4 cm

4 cm

Perimeter:

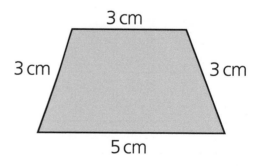

3 cm

3 cm

3 cm

5 cm

Perimeter:

63

Perimeter of rectangles and squares

1. Perimeter of a rectangle

a. Perimeter of a swimming pool

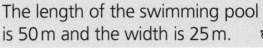 The length of the swimming pool is 50 m and the width is 25 m.

 What's the perimeter of the swimming pool?

Add the four sides together.

50 + 25 + 50 + 25

= ⬛ m

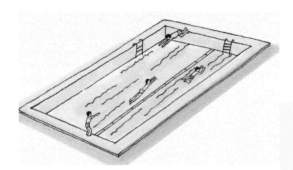

 I'll add 2 lengths to 2 widths.

2 × 50 + 2 × 25

= ⬛

= ⬛ m

The sum of two lots of 'width plus length'.

2 × (50 + 25)

= ⬛

= ⬛ m

Answer: ⬛⬛⬛⬛⬛⬛

b. Find the perimeter of each rectangle.

12 m | 24 m

Number sentence:

Answer:

25 m | 55 m

Number sentence:

Answer:

 Let's summarise how to calculate the perimeter of a rectangle.

The perimeter of a rectangle:
⬛ × (length + width)

2. Perimeter of a square

a. Perimeter of a square-shaped table

The length of each side is 120 cm.

Think about it. How can we calculate the perimeter of a square-shaped table?

I'll add the four sides together.

As the lengths of all four sides are the same, I'll use multiplication.

120 + 120 + 120 + 120

= ▢ cm

4 × 120

= ▢ cm

Answer: ▢

b. Find the perimeter of each square.

18 m

25 m

Number sentence:

Answer:

Number sentence:

Answer:

Let's summarise how to calculate the perimeter of a square.

The perimeter of a square:

▢ × side length

3. Simple research

Use lolly sticks to make shapes.

Lots of shapes can be made using 12 lolly sticks.

How many lolly sticks are needed for the perimeter of each of these shapes? /

What is the area of each shape measured in squares of lolly sticks? ☐

Which shape is the largest?

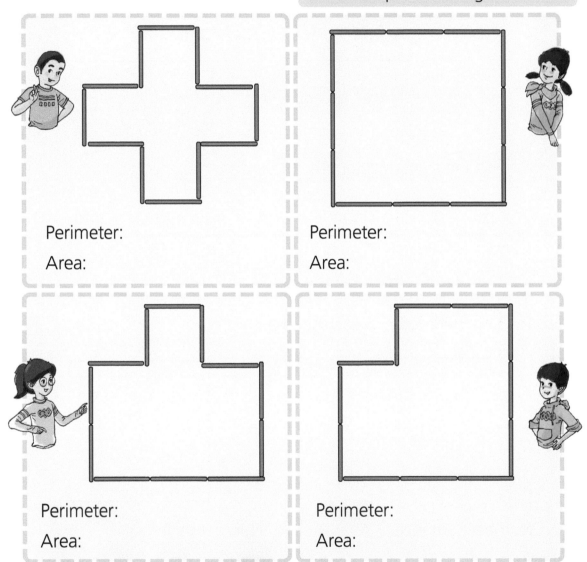

Perimeter:

Area:

Perimeter:

Area:

Perimeter:

Area:

Perimeter:

Area:

What have you discovered?

We have found that, when the perimeters of the shapes are the same, the areas are ▮▮▮▮▮▮▮▮.

Unit Seven
Consolidating and enhancing

Multiplication and division

1. a. Write your own calculation problems, multiplying two-digit numbers by other two-digit numbers. Choose the numbers from the four number cards below.

Estimate the answers first. Then calculate the exact answers.
Which calculation problem produces the smallest number?
Which calculation problem produces the greatest number?

b. Use the column method to complete these calculations.
Then check your answers using a calculator.

82 × 65 =   93 × 59 =   75 × 650 =   120 × 790 =

734 × 56 =   431 × 47 =   705 × 65 =   400 × 230 =

c. Complete these calculations, writing out each step of the process. Then check your answers using a calculator.

149 + 55 × 24   65 × 35 – 1668   3264 ÷ 8 × 70

2. a.

I have a division question for you: 298 ÷ 3☐ = ?
Choose a number from the number cards on the right to put in the box and form a calculation where a three-digit number is divided by a two-digit number. Try with each of the number cards.

b.

Put 1, 3 and 4, respectively, in the ☐, and then calculate ☐98 ÷ 39. Are the numbers of digits of the quotients the same? Estimate first, and then calculate the answer exactly.

198 ÷ 39 =

398 ÷ 39 =

498 ÷ 39 =

c. Use the column method to complete these calculations.
Check your answers.

728 ÷ 56 =   4110 ÷ 47 =   6554 ÷ 65 =

69

3. Complete these calculations, writing out each step of the process. Then check your answers using a calculator.

372 + 518 ÷ 14   8007 − 1680 ÷ 12   465 ÷ 15 × 28

25 × (281 + 43)   3774 ÷ (100 − 63)   5400 ÷ (1890 ÷ 21)

Did you know?

A long time ago, people carried out multiplications by using a 'grid calculation' method. This method was described by Cheng Dawei, in a *Complete Collection of Algorithms*. He called this method 'the grid method'. 47 × 35 is calculated in his book like this:

47 × 35 = ▇

```
        3   5
      1 | 2
      2 |   0   4
      2 | 3
        1 |     5   7
    1   6   4   5
```

```
      4 7
  ×   3 5
  -------
      3 5
    2 0 0
    2 1 0
  1 2 0 0
  -------
  1 6 4 5
```

2 + 2 + 2   0 + 3 + 1

Fractions

1. The fractions represent the shaded parts of the images.
Are they correct? Decide 'yes' or 'no' for each image.

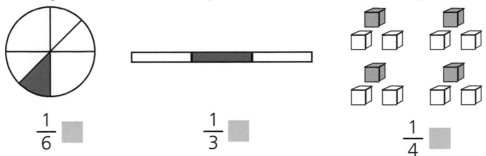

$\frac{1}{6}$ ▢ $\frac{1}{3}$ ▢ $\frac{1}{4}$ ▢

2. Colour a part of each picture for the fractions given.

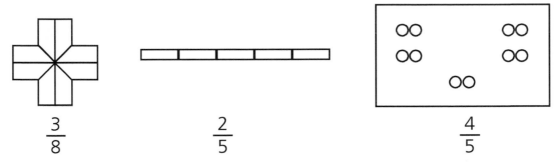

$\frac{3}{8}$ $\frac{2}{5}$ $\frac{4}{5}$

3. Write fractions to represent the red part in each diagram below.

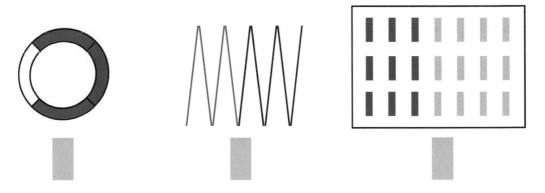

4. Copy the pictures. Circle $\frac{1}{4}$ of the items in each picture.

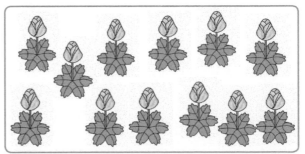

Problem solving

1. The playground in Forest Park is a rectangle with a length of 150 metres and a width of 88 metres. What is its area?

2. 987 pupils want to visit Forest Park. If one coach can take 48 pupils, how many coaches will they need?

3. One ticket for entry to Forest Park is £12. If more people go, it's better to buy a group ticket. 160 pupils visited the park and paid £1280 for the group ticket. How much cheaper per person was the group ticket?

4. The bear that lives in Forest Park has a mass of 69 kilograms. The elephant that lives in the park has a mass that is 76 times the mass of the bear. What is the mass of the elephant?

5. A panda eats 18 kilograms of food a day. The amount of food eaten by the elephant is 8 kilograms more than 19 times the amount eaten by the panda. How much food does the elephant eat a day?

6. A squirrel packs 42 pinecones into each pot. 273 pots have been packed, and 798 pinecones haven't been packed. How many pots will the squirrel pack in total?

7. Dylan and Emma walk for 84 minutes from the entrance to the exit of Forest Park. If their walking speed is 38 m/min, what is the distance from the entrance to the exit? Alex and Poppy walk the same distance in 76 minutes. What is their walking speed?

Perimeter and area

1. a. If you use a rope to make a rectangle with an area of 512 m² and a length of 32 m, how long is the rope?

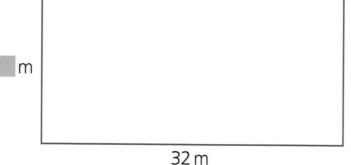

If we know the length and the width of the rectangle, we can calculate its perimeter.

☐ m

32 m

Calculate the width of the rectangle first:

Then calculate the perimeter of the rectangle:

Answer:

b. If you make a square with the same length of rope, what is the area of the square?

As long as we know the length of the sides, we can calculate the area.

Answer:

2. The area of this rectangle is 2350 m².
What is its perimeter?

25 m

☐ m

Maths amusement park – Who can make the rectangle with the largest area?

Make rectangles (including squares) with 20 lolly sticks.

Let's see who makes the rectangle with the largest area.

Let's try it out! Use 20 lolly sticks to make various rectangles and squares.

Maths amusement park – Combinations

Example 1

The school football team has three colours of shirt and two colours of shorts.

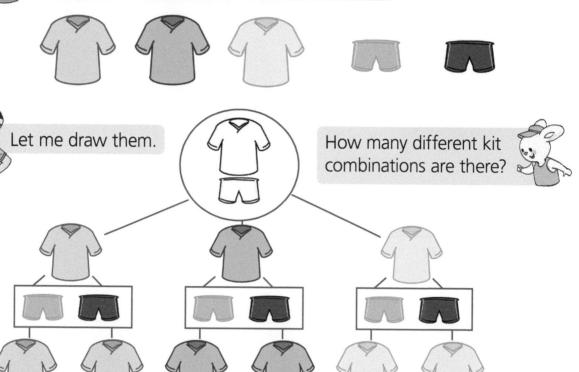

Let me draw them.

How many different kit combinations are there?

There are 6 different kit combinations in total.

We can also draw it like this.

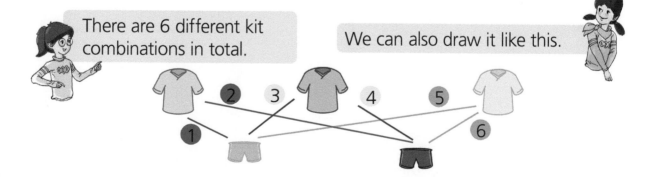

Practice

Each person selects one meat dish and one vegetable dish. How many possible combinations are there?

Meat dishes	**Vegetable dishes**
Fried chicken	Fried vegetables
Braised beef	Boiled cabbage
Lamb chop	Tofu
Beef stew	

Example 2

Some pupils are making lanterns out of red and green paper.

Each lantern has three layers and each layer is either red or green.

How many different combinations are there? Finish colouring in the diagram below.

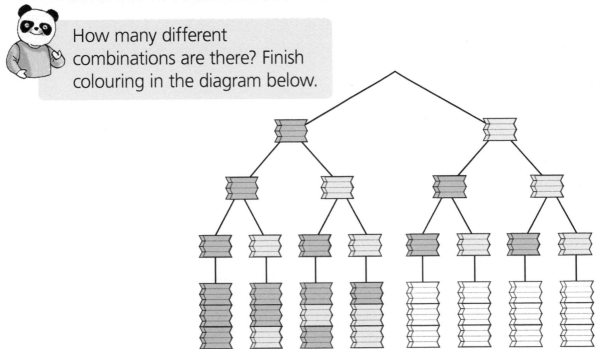

Maths amusement park – Counting

1. How many oranges are there in the picture? How many calculation methods could you use to find out? Write the number sentences.

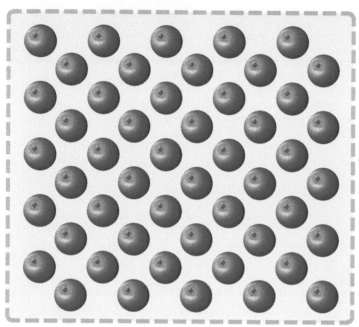

Count them one by one. However, it takes ages and it's easy to make mistakes!

Count them in groups!

Count them in tens!

Count them diagonally!

2. Equilateral triangles with sides of 1 cm have been combined to make one large equilateral triangle.

    a. How many equilateral triangles with sides of 1 cm are there?

    b. How many equilateral triangles with sides of 2 cm are there?

How can we count them without missing any?

I divide them into two kinds of triangle, those pointing upwards ($\triangle$) and those pointing downwards ($\triangledown$). Then I can count them!

Maths amusement park – Putting apples in drawers

1. Dylan, Emma, Poppy and Alex are putting apples in drawers.

Put 3 apples into 2 drawers. No matter how they divide the apples, one drawer always has more apples than the other.

2. What if they tried putting 4 apples into 3 drawers?

What would they find?